C

W

FR

D1326436

The Magic of
Celtic Spirituality

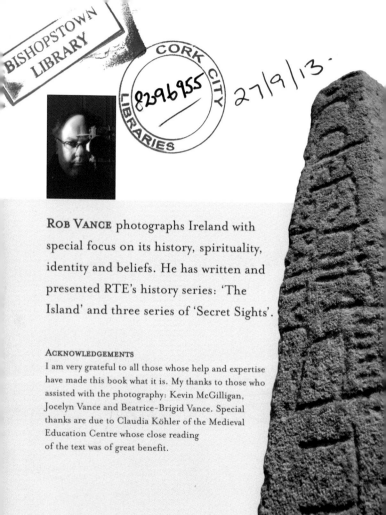

ROB VANCE photographs Ireland with
special focus on its history, spirituality,
identity and beliefs. He has written and
presented RTE's history series: 'The
Island' and three series of 'Secret Sights'.

ACKNOWLEDGEMENTS

I am very grateful to all those whose help and expertise
have made this book what it is. My thanks to those who
assisted with the photography: Kevin McGilligan,
Jocelyn Vance and Beatrice-Brigid Vance. Special
thanks are due to Claudia Köhler of the Medieval
Education Centre whose close reading
of the text was of great benefit.

THE MAGIC OF

Celtic Spirituality

ROB VANCE

THE O'BRIEN PRESS
DUBLIN

First published 2006 by The O'Brien Press Ltd,
12 Terenure Road East, Rathgar, Dublin 6, Ireland.
Tel: +353 1 4923333; Fax: +353 1 4922777
E-mail: books@obrien.ie
Website: www.obrien.ie

ISBN-10: 0-86278-932-X
ISBN-13: 978-0-86278-932-9
Copyright for text and illustrations
© Rob Vance 2006

Poem p10 translated by James Carney

British Library Cataloguing-in-Publication Data
Vance, Robert
Magic of Celtic spirituality
1.Magic, Celtic 2.Celts – Religion
3.Sacred space – Ireland
I.Title
299.1'6

1 2 3 4 5 6 7 8 9 10
06 07 08 09

Printed and bound in Poland. Produced by Polskabook.

CONTENTS

INTRODUCTION

Celtic Spirituality is many things: a time frame, a
mode of spiritual understanding and perhaps a
personal encounter in a place of ancient wisdom.
       This book is about places in Ireland that facilitate
that encounter.

As a philosophy, Celtic Spirituality is a fusion, a harking-
back to a time when churches were simple timber
structures surrounded by nature. Saints healed the sick, but
were known to cast spells on a bad day. It was a time when
a pagan virgin priestess could be baptised as a Christian,
but continue as before, bringing more into the fold of the
new religion. It was a time when nature was still holy.

Since the time of the burial mounds, the peoples of this
island sought communion with the unknown world of the
spirit. Many of the early tombs resemble great stone bellies,

symbolic mothers receiving the dead into their maternal bodies. The power of the goddess gave life and creativity to all, but confrontation developed as Christianity gradually began to centre on an exclusively male priesthood.

But to the people of ancient Ireland, nature was female; goddess, maiden, cailleach – witch or wise woman – were all part of nature. She was seen as a Great Mother, a triple-goddess like Kar, who gave the words 'carnal' and 'karma'. She appears in Ireland as Anu, whose great breasts thrust from the Kerry landscape and whose voluptuous hill is south of Lough Gur in Limerick. If we eat a cereal, we remember her name as Ceres, the goddess of the crop. As a deity, she was the mysterious root of growth and change, the eternal silence from which everything emerges and to which everything returns.

But gradually across Europe, as warfare and aggression increased, the female gods were relegated to the edges of belief as more

masculine gods came to the fore.

By the fifth century AD, the writings of eastern mystics, in combination with Egyptian and Syrian asceticism, introduced new spiritual ideas to Christianity. Concurrently, as the Roman Empire collapsed, confidence in a state that could guarantee law and order collapsed also. For many monks, society could no longer offer a secure life, so they sought a desert, a place where contemplation and prayer could grant access to heavenly grace. They went as far west as they could, bringing a new aesthetic of contemplation to a remote island in the ocean – the island that became known as Ireland.

On that island, an ancient people, part Bronze Age, part Celtic, evolved a complex agrarian society, complete with a humane legal system, rich oral culture and ruling warrior elite, similar to the Samurai of ancient Japan. They were sophisticated, traded with Gaul and Iberia and were familiar with many philosophies of the East. The kings of Ireland gave land to the early saints as many of their sons and daughters joined the Christian religion. As these converts became fluent in Latin, they created a mixture of nature and the numinous in their poetry and literature, suggesting a surreal blend of the normal and supernatural. To those early Christian poets, transcendence could be found in a flower or in the contemplation of a sunrise. The natural world expressed the creativity of the power that ruled all:

> There sings to me the cuckoo
> From bush-citadels in grey hood.
> God's doom! May the Lord protect me
> Writing well, under the grey wood.

In the opening centuries of the Christian era, the churches of the first Christians replaced the oak groves as sacred centres and the modes and rituals of the old religion were replaced and ultimately forgotten, to remain as folk wisdom in the countryside. As Christianity replaced paganism, the 'old religion' symbol of the serpent reappeared on crosiers, bells and manuscripts; baptism with water was seen by the Irish as a borrowing from their own rituals, using water as a symbol of life; the Son of God replaced the Sun.

As a form of worship, Celtic Spirituality refers back to that early Church and its affinity with the natural world. Early Christianity was a profound attempt to create an agreed 'sense of the world', as monks and nuns became symbols of the ideal that every human being had universal and equivalent value and that access to the divine was open to all. They preached a captivating blend of biblical knowledge and eastern mysticism, as well as the good business idea of granting retrospective heavenly bliss to the ancestors of anyone who gave land for a monastery.

But in today's terms, Celtic Spirituality is something that should be experienced, not merely 'understood'. Its esoteric mood exists at a sublime level. At the sites associated with holy men and women in Ireland it is not unusual to become aware of the uncanny, as inner subjectivity replaces the twenty-first century and its techno-clamour. Opening to this experience is what Celtic Spirituality is about.

So while being neither part of mainstream Christianity, nor

contemporary paganism, Celtic Spirituality tolerates and utilises both. It stands as a challenge to the materialism of contemporary society and celebrates the uniqueness and inherent divinity of each individual, seeing in the body of the mother the same spark as the body of the father.

The intention of this book is to reveal some of these holy places and allow more people to share their unique atmosphere and sense of spiritual renewal.

HOLY WELLS

any wells began their existence as outlets of the Sacred Feminine where the healing balm of Anu, the great earth goddess, could be found. The wells were the original 'Holy Water' and many continue to have that function in a Christian context, while some hold celebrations known as 'pattern days' when elaborate prayerful circuits of the well are made. There is often a 'rag-tree' where pieces of cloth, toys or coins are left as offerings. The wells represent an unbroken tradition of Celtic Spirituality stretching back 1,500 years.

WATERSTOWN, CO. CARLOW

This lonely spot was a pilgrim site in the early Christian centuries. Little is known about the cross and wooded mound, but a pilgrim track runs back toward Rathvilly. The well, which is a weathered bullaun stone, is set into the wall opposite the cross.

ST PATRICK'S WELL, DUBLIN

Hidden behind the wall of Trinity College as it runs along Nassau Street, the ancient well of St Patrick dates to the fifth century and was part of the Priory of the Holy Trinity. It can be reached by applying to the Provost's House.

ST MOLAISE'S WELL, OLD LEIGHLIN, CO. CARLOW

This holy well has a small wheeled cross with rags and offerings attached. It sits within the precincts of Old Leighlin, a small hamlet, and was originally beside one of Ireland's sacred trees, the Yew of Ross. When the old tree fell in the seventh

century, its wood was shared out between various saints and made into church roof shingles and boxes for relics. April 18th is St Molaise's day and his well is the site for a 'pattern' or prayer gathering.

LOUGH INNE EYE WELL, CO. CORK

The approach to this well is through tall woodland. The path meanders through buttercups and marigolds, but on a cloudy day, one wanders through murky darkness. The well and its rag tree are a sudden start of vibrant colour in the shadows.

UISNEACH, CO. WESTMEATH

The Hill of Uisneach is one of the least-known sacred sites in Ireland despite its important place in pre-history as a centre of druidic activity. There is a huge boulder on its southern slope, 'The Catstone', representing the navel of Ireland and beside it is a secluded hawthorn copse, which hides the well.

BALLYVOURNEY, CO. CORK

This well is associated with the sixth-century saint, Gobnait, the patron of bees, her name deriving from Deborah, the Hebrew for 'Honey Bee'. She found the spot for her monastery having been

given a dream of nine white deer. She saw the deer at Ballyvourney and knew it was the place.

She was granted the land, founded a religious community of women, and began tending the sick and poor. She is reputed to have kept a plague from Ballyvourney through an incantation.

ST BRIGID'S WELL, LISCANNOR, CO. CLARE

This is a place of healing and encouragement. Entering the tunnel-like chamber, one is aware of the ageless appeal of St Brigid. The water flows noisily into a stone basin set in the ground, which is surrounded by pictures of children and several of firemen killed in the September 11 attacks. Discarded crutches testify to her enduring appeal to those in need. It is considered especially lucky to see a fish in the well as this guarantees that prayers will be answered.

Nunneries

From the sixth century, women in Christian Europe and in Ireland began to take the veil and become nuns. Several were probably Celtic female druids who adopted the 'new' religion and while records of their foundations are scant, some were important. Most have disappeared completely or become part of later all-male settlements.

KILLEEDY, CO. LIMERICK

This was founded by St Ita, who had the glorious title 'The White Sun of the Women of Munster'. She kept a school attended by, among others, St Brendan the navigator. A lullaby in which she sings to the infant Jesus is attributed to her:

Jesueen I nurse in my little hermitage.
All is a lie but Jesueen –
Even though it were a priest with great wealth...

LADY'S ISLAND, CO. WEXFORD

This popular pilgrimage site is an island in a large saltwater lagoon, reached by a small causeway across the mudflats. Its Irish name, *Cluain na mBan*, means 'Meadow of the Women'. There are several raths visible beneath the grassy meadow behind the church, and a statue of the Blessed Virgin faces the sea at the far end of the island.

Tradition maintains that it was a pagan site in antiquity – the area was renowned for sun worship and the 'women' in the name of the island were probably druids. It seems likely that the coming of St Abban Christianised these women and their dedication was switched to the Virgin Mary. On the western side of the island is a tiny holy well, which may have been the original used by the female druids before Christianity.

THE NUNS CHURCH, CLONMACNOISE, CO. OFFALY

This entrance arch, part of the ruined monastic settlement of Clonmacnoise is the entrance to a Romanesque church built towards the end of the twelfth century by a repentant queen of reputedly great beauty. Her affair with a neighbouring prince brought the Anglo-Normans to Ireland, beginning a challenging era in Irish history. Queen Dervorgilla retired here after taking holy orders. The arch to her church has a motif of animals gnawing a vine, while the capitals are adorned with terrifying heads. The church stands just beside the main buildings of Clonmacnoise – the water meadow of Naoise – founded by St Ciaran in 548 AD. Like Iona in Scotland, it is the burial place of many Irish kings and princes such as O'Meolaghlin of Meath, O'Conor Don of Connaught, O'Kelly, MacCarthy Mór, McDermot and others.

ST BRIGID'S MONASTERY, CO. KILDARE

The town of Kildare – *Cill Dara*, church of the oak wood – came to prominence through the endeavours of its native saint, Brigid of 'the Fiery Arrow', the most popular saint in Ireland after Saint Patrick.

Brigid was perhaps the best known of the individuals who were both pagan and Christian, and who were venerated by both traditions. She has been identified with Brigantia, a Celtic tribal goddess and may have been a pagan priestess with a retinue of virgins who became a convert to Christianity. Her legendary goodness and enduring spiritual vitality enabled her shrine and sacred flame to survive the closure of the monasteries under Henry VIII and it only succumbed to destruction under Cromwell in 1649.

The remains of the fire house where the eternal flame was kept are visible beside the Romanesque cathedral that stands on the site of her oak-grove. It is more than possible that the remains of her pagan temple lie beneath the floor of the present building.

Today, the round tower of the monastery and her holy well endure and are visited and prayed at all year round. Special attention is paid to her feast day of 1 February, the start of spring and the Celtic festival of Imbolc, when it was said that ewes begin to lactate. In many parts of the country, 'straw babies' were left outside cottages on Brigid's eve until they were 'invited' in by the families, thereby making 'Brigid' welcome. She is recorded as having died in 525 AD and, according to tradition, her remains lie at the side of the altar in the cathedral in Kildare town.

EARLY CHURCHES
& MONASTERIES

The early churches tended to be built away from people, to allow for undisturbed contemplation. Most were built for the personal religious use of the monks; prayers and psalms, remote and silent. Other more missionary monks and nuns became established on major routeways, near to the high-status ring forts of their royal patrons.

In general, the chieftains gave the land for the monasteries, granting land sufficient to carry sheep, but as their popularity grew, many churches became centres of population and practically proto-towns by the time of the Norse arrivals.

The monasteries were accepted by Celtic society,

offering a form of tribal kinship so essential to that culture. The abbot or abbess was a type of chieftain, and the monks or nuns like adopted fosterlings. The spiritual leaders fulfilled many of the ancient roles formerly held by the priestly caste of druids and bards.

Young Celtic aristocrats became attracted to the new religion and many of the Church's most able and gifted leaders came from this class, such as St Declan and St Colmcille, both fusions of warrior and saint.

MONAINCHA, CO. OFFALY

Sitting high on a landlocked island in a formerly extensive bog, this sixth-century foundation is especially peaceful and quiet. Far from any road or highway and usually deserted, it offers an especially silent place for contemplation.

The fine Romanesque carvings of the chancel arch, though just discernable, are high in quality. There is also a small high cross. Male desire was a major source of distraction to the monks, causing them to threaten a magic spell that any woman or female animal would 'die immediately' upon entering the island!

GALLEN, CO. OFFALY

Gallen, founded in 492, was on an important routeway through the bogs of county Offaly. This ancient route followed the well-drained Brosna valley and ran along the north side of the river for a considerable distance from Gallen to St Managhan's Church. Gallen itself has a fine collection of Early Christian cross-slabs, many attached to the church on the site. Just north of the monastery between The Doon and

Ballycumber another trackway runs along the south side of the existing road and between the two trails are several high-status ringforts, the residences of the local '*tighern*' or lord and his 'palace guard'. He and his immediate family would have granted land to the monastery, making sure that the monks remained on the lower ground, suitable for tillage, but not for cattle.

SEIRKEIRAN, CO. OFFALY

This monastic site of over ten acres still retains traces of the surrounding earthen wall and defensive ditch. The wall, rising in places to six metres in height, gives a sense of the defended nature of the settlement. St Ciaran the Elder, 'first-born of the Saints of Ireland' founded the monastery sometime in the fifth century on heavily forested lands granted by the local dynasty; 'St Ciaran's Tree' can be seen overleaf. Ciaran was an interesting saint – he wore the skins of animals and had as his first monks a badger, a fox, a wolf and a deer. St Ciaran went on to use his abilities in a more profitable manner and became the owner of 'large herds of cattle' according to the *Feilire Oengusso*, a mediaeval Irish commentary on the lives of saints. There are more than twenty ring forts in the area, connected to each other and to the high status forts by a trackway that runs to the east of the monastic enclosure. Adjacent to the site is a now

obliterated ring-fort, probably the main residence of the local chieftain, which formed part of a series of visually connected ring-forts of differing functions – defence, farming and habitation – which formed the nuclei of the '*tuath*' or tribal territory.

CLONMORE MONASTIC SITE & CROSSES, CO. CARLOW

This small monastery has so many saints interred in its small burial ground it is known as the Angelic Cemetery.

It was founded by St Maedhog, a scion of a Leinster dynasty who struck down an ancient tree on the site when it was a pagan sancuary. He was roundly berated by 'the women of the trumpet song', perhaps the druidic guardians of Clonmore. The graveyard has many early crosses and a huge triple bullaun stone sits beside a stream close by.

MOVILLA, CO. DOWN

This mainly medieval site, whose name comes from *Magh Bile* or 'Plain of the Great Tree', was founded in the sixth century by St Finnian on what had been a pagan site of some importance. *The Penitential of St Finnian* states that 'if a woman by her magic destroys the child she has conceived, she shall do penance for half a year', however if she keeps the child the penance will be six years, as the sin is now public. After six years of penance, St Finnian considered that the woman's virginity was now restored!

ST AUDEON'S CHURCH, DUBLIN

In the porch of this recently restored Anglican Church, there is an incised Christian stone, perhaps an early grave-slab. It has been there since the eighth century, when St Brendan built a timber church on the site, marking the beginning of the *Slighe Mhór*, the 'great road' to the monastery of Clonmacnoise and points further west. Pilgrims leaving on the long trek would touch the stone and pray for a safe journey. As they murmured their prayers, they may have repeated the ancient saying, '*Teanga na dia thungus mo thuath*', 'I swear by the god my people swear by', for the older pagan beliefs continued into the Christian era and the general word for a god, '*dia*' was used for pagan and Christian deity alike.

INISCEALTRA, CO. CLARE

[BOAT FROM SCARIFF]

Founded on an island on Lough Derg by St Caimin in the seventh century, the monastery was burnt by Vikings in 836 and 922. The Benedictines were established on the island by the latter date and the island remained a monastery until the end of the sixteenth century. It is an extraordinary place, retaining an air of peace and tranquillity quite unspoiled by any development. The last witch of Lough Derg, reputedly a convert to Christianity, is buried within the nave of St Caimin's Church.

GLENDALOUGH, CO. WICKLOW

This popular site, whose name translates as 'The Glen of Two Lakes', is subject to mass invasion by coaches and cameras during the tourist season, but is worth visiting on misty or otherwise inclement days. The monastery was founded by St Kevin in the sixth century and has several interesting buildings and remains, including St Kevin's Bed, a manmade cave above the upper lake and St Kevin's Kitchen, a twelfth-century church. The original monastery was situated around the shore of the upper lake, but the monks moved down the valley around the tenth century when numbers increased and more buildings were needed.

According to tradition, the treasure of Glendalough — books, altar silverware and a shrine — was moved when the Vikings first attacked and has never been found. Folklore suggests it was buried somewhere between the valley and Glenmalure, and as those responsible for its hurried concealment were killed by marauders, it may lie there still.

KILLESHIN, CO. LAOIS

This atmospheric monastic site was established in the fifth century by St Comghan and produced several notable saints of the early Christian Church, including St Aodhan and St Diarmait. Comghan's birth was said to have been attended by women followers of the old religion who were versed in midwifery. The door of the present church is one of the finest pieces of Scandinavian 'Urnes' stonework in Ireland, having foliage, scrollwork and heads with intertwined hair and swirling moustaches.

CLONMACNOISE, CO. OFFALY

This great monastery, founded by St Ciaran, was endowed with land by the O'Conor kings of Connacht from its inception in the sixth century. It quickly became a market as well as a monastery and school, and merchants from Gaul and the Mediterranean are recorded as visiting and trading with the Irish and the monks. Wine was popular, and Irish wool and hides were commodities much in demand in Europe. Its cathedral was robbed by a farm-worker about a hundred years after its foundation and the Annals of the Four Masters recorded 'the theft of a silver model of Solomon's Temple, a silver cup, a silver drinking horn, a silver chalice, a paten and other objects', presumably all expensive gifts from the O'Conors whose kings were traditionally buried at the monastery. St Ciaran's foundation grew into the greatest of all the Irish monasteries and had a school, teaching the works of Virgil, Horace and Ovid, and the scriptures. It drew students from Britannia and Gaul, but unfortunately it also attracted the greed of the Vikings and they plundered the monastery in 834, 835 and 842. The site still has beautiful high crosses and a superb collection of almost four hundred decorated grave slabs, dating back to the sixth and seventh centuries.

CLONFERT CATHEDRAL, CO. GALWAY

Founded by St Brendan in 563, this church has the finest Romanesque doorway in Ireland. The twelfth-century facade is decorated with what appear to be decapitated stone heads, as if the Celtic custom, or perhaps, 'motif', of decorating their houses with the heads of slain enemies, as symbols of virility and prowess in war, remained on ... at least in architectural terms.

The amazingly intricate doorcase consists of animals gnawing tendrils, wild foliage and strange glowering faces, while the singular heads, perhaps recalling benefactors of the church, are displayed like a china collection above the door.

In 838 the abbot of this church was unwilling to retaliate

against the Vikings who were pillaging monasteries across the south of the country and instead robbed Clonmacnois and Durrow himself! He was finally struck dead in 847 by an angry curse from St Ciaran. The Great Navigator, St Brendan, is said to be buried in the churchyard.

INISMURRAY, CO. SLIGO
[BOAT FROM MULLAGHMORE]

This beautiful island lies out in the Atlantic, four miles north-west of Streedagh point in County Sligo. The monastery was founded by St Molaise of Killala in the sixth century and the island had a viable community until 1948. The fierce Atlantic storms did not deter the Vikings who burnt the monastery in 802. A group of cursing stones

placed there subsequently to render a hurt to the northmen, remain; they must have been effective, since there were no further raids on the island!

This unique monastery has a massive surrounding stone wall and contains beehive huts, a primitive church with a Greek cross on its lintel and several other buildings relating to its founding saint. One of these, Teampuill-na-teinead, the 'Church of the Fire', had a perpetual fire burning in a central hearth, night and day with a monk detailed to make sure it was never extinguished.

TULLYLEASE, CO. CORK

The monastery was founded by St Berrihert; he lived there with a female companion, a sister who remained a virgin. This was not unusual, many Irish and Saxon saints had female companions whose equal opportunity to perform the sacraments was accepted in the early Church. Tullylease contains the finest Early Christian grave slab in the country, whose ninth-century inscription reads; '*Quicumque Legerit Hunc Titulum Orat Pro Berechtuir*'

– 'Whoever reads this inscription, let him pray for Berichter'.

KILMALKEDAR, CO. KERRY

This ancient monastic site was established by St Maolcathair, a noted saint who died in the year 636. The chancel arch and the roof truss with its animal decorations are excellent examples of the Romanesque style. Outside, there is a sundial marked into the sections of the monastic day and an Ogham stone dedicated to Mael Inber, son of Brocan.

SKELLIG MICHAEL, CO. KERRY

This dramatic rock soars 700 feet above the heaving and grey Atlantic and has a collection of monastic cells and a small oratory. By tradition a pagan site dedicated to Manannan Mac Lir, the god of the sea, it was 're-baptised' as Skellig Michael sometime in the seventh century. The monks came to this barren rock and built two small

churches, a number of circular beehive dwellings and an
oratory. In boats made of hide they transported enough soil
for a garden, and their own graves.

GALLARUS ORATORY,
CO. KERRY

A perfectly preserved oratory
perhaps from the eleventh century
or earlier, shaped as an upturned
boat and offering a dark
contemplative space for saint
and sinner alike.

ST BERRIHERT'S KYLE, CO. TIPPERARY

This unknown and secret monk's arbour is one of the most hidden and sacred places in Ireland. It retains an atmosphere of almost tangible sanctity amid its lush surroundings. The monks who lived here are buried nearby and their curious circular 'church' contains many early Christian crosses and religious symbols. It is dominated by a large oak tree, perhaps part of the original Aherlow woods, and a high cross, set into the wall and of unusual decoration. The route to the hermitage is across a boggy daffodil-filled field, and through a natural gateway of two hawthorn bushes.

High Crosses,
Inscribed Stones &
Stone Carvings

The Celtic High Cross, using biblical imagery together with Christ's passion, became the ultimate icon of Irish Christianity. Although they are Christian, many of the bewildering range of scenes on the crosses remain enigmatic, chosen perhaps for spiritual and symbolic meaning rather than a systematic explanation of the bible and its characters. In total, over ninety separate subjects have been identified on Ireland's high crosses and each cross uses a different selection of these motifs. They were probably commissioned by local kings and monastic rulers as a way of proclaiming their own authority and status.

They may even have had a semi-magical role as prayers fixed in stone, an everlasting celestial discourse. It is possible that specific Christian rituals took place around the cross at special times; given that archaeologists believe they were painted in vivid colours, their effect would have been striking.

The crosses were usually positioned at the cardinal points of the monastery, limiting the perimeter and the holy ground within. Harpers, saints, animals, biblical scenes and Celtic scrollwork are typical motifs of the crosses still in good condition.

OLD KILCULLEN, CO. KILDARE

This windswept hill has the fragmentary remains of a monastery founded by St Patrick in the fifth century. As well as the remains of a round tower, it contains the bases of several high crosses, one in particular having good detail of biblical scenes, including Samson wrestling with the lion and other unidentified religious or secular cameos. It enjoyed almost five hundred years of uninterrupted occupation until the Viking raids of the tenth century.

MOONE, CO. KILDARE

The tallest high cross in Ireland is in Moone, and it stands near a site named after a sacred Yew tree. It is an exquisite piece of ninth-century carving and may represent an artistic revival of  an earlier, pagan tradition. While the granite panels contain biblical scenes, including Daniel and the lions, and the story of the loaves and the fishes, their carving style and method of display have a mesmeric quality, as strange doll-like figures gaze expressionless from the panels like toys caught in stone. This enigmatic work of art, almost inducing an aesthetic trance, seems more Christian totem pole than high cross and may have replaced the original sacred object, the Yew.

MONASTERBOICE, CO. LOUTH

Founded in the fifth century by a St Buite, who has remained in obscurity, this monastic site contains two of the finest high crosses in Ireland, both dating to the ninth century.

KINNITY, CO. OFFALY

A small monastic settlement existed here from the sixth century, when St Finian Cam founded a monastery in what were the great woods of the Sliabh Blooms. This area was always important for spiritual needs and in Celtic times, Fionn MacCumhall came to this area to be cared for by Lia Luachra and Bomhall, two female seers.

The cross was erected at the wish of Colman Maelsechnaill, High King of Ireland from 846-862, and is decorated with interlacing, scenes of Adam and Eve, and birds.

KILLADEAS, CO. FERMANAGH

The undated 'Bishop's Stone' stands in a small graveyard off the B82 from Enniskillen. The figure is just over a metre high and suggests a somewhat melancholy cleric, perhaps overly fond of the good life and now full of regret. The carving is curved to fit the shape of the stone and shows both relief and full face of the unknown ecclesiastic, a figure evoking sympathy.

KILNARUANE, CO. CORK

This standing stone (previous page) has a rugged strength that suits its position near Bantry Bay. It has carvings of a cross, praying figures, animals, interlacing and a boat with four oarsmen. It is quite a contrast to the urbane crosses of the midlands. As it is not visited by coaches or crowds, it retains a sense of private encounter.

AHENNY, CO. TIPPERARY

The eighth-century crosses at Ahenny, or more accurately St Cuthbert's Church, are decorated with a variety of scrolls and bosses, suggesting a development from earlier wooden versions. They are stylistically similar to the artwork in the Book of Kells and are executed in a robust and confident manner. The north cross, which had, until the 1960s, extraordinary scenes of animals and funeral processions, is now entirely unreadable, due to a form of lichenous decay of the stone.

FAHAN CROSS, CO. DONEGAL

The village of Fahan lies just over

four miles south of Buncrana and is home to one of the finest examples of early Christian art in Ulster. There was a monastery here in the seventh century, founded by St Mura. The cross has superb stone carvings and interlacings. The inscription on the north edge of the cross reads (in Latin) 'Glory and Honour to the Father and the Son and the Holy Ghost', part of a prayer first approved by the council of Toledo in 633.

DYSERT O'DEA, CO. CLARE

Founded in the early eighth century by St Tola, the church has twelfth-century heads carved around a doorcase, their bluish limestone features still crisp after nine

hundred years! There is also a round tower and the shaft of a twelfth-century high cross with a striking interlace design of serpents and foliage. It lacks the connecting ring of earlier high crosses, but has a boldly carved crucifixion and a representation of a bishop.

KELLS, CO. MEATH

This historic town has existed in one form or another since the sixth century. It lies in the partly wooded valley of the Blackwater, and it was in the monastery here that portions of the world-famous Book of Kells were so beautifully illuminated. This book, arguably

the finest piece of illuminated art ever produced, is now on display in Trinity College, Dublin. Kells remained a wealthy and powerful monastery despite repeated attacks from Vikings and Irish kings and grew into an important walled town in the middle ages. There are five crosses around the site, dating from the eighth to the eleventh centuries, showing a wide range of biblical scenes. The market cross has a frieze of animals, including a centaur, around its base.

BEALIN, CO. WESTMEATH

This ninth-century cross has an interesting collection of carvings showing animals with bird-like heads, similar to the fantastic animals on the base of the high cross at Moone in Kildare. Bealin's cross has a scroll of coiled animals and hunting scenes showing mounted riders and a hound and is probably part of a series of crosses related to Tuathgal, Abbot of Clonmacnoise, who died in 811.

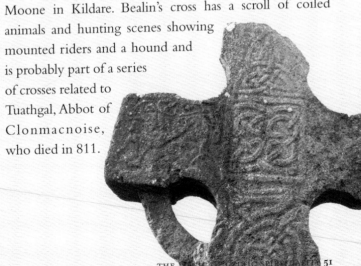

DURROW, CO. OFFALY

Durrow's fine high cross sits in the woodland amid the graves of Donal, King of Tara, Murchadh, grandson of Brian Boru, and other kings, whose tombstones were probably destroyed by Hugh de Lacy in 1186. Durrow is, of course, celebrated for The Book of Durrow, one of the earliest Christian manuscripts, probably created around the

year 680. Durrow was a renowned centre of culture and learning in the Dark Ages, when its monks travelled across Europe bringing scripture and classical philosophy to the continent.

KILNASAGGART, CO. ARMAGH

Just over the border and beside the railway line is the Cross Pillar of Kilnasaggart, which dates from about 700 AD. Its inscription translated from Irish reads; 'Ternoc, son of Little Ceran bequeaths this place under the protection of St Peter'. The pillar has thirteen crosses inscribed on its two metre length and stands near the ancient prehistoric routeway into Ulster.

SHEELA-NA-GIGS

Found on walls, churches and other buildings, Sheela-na-Gigs are stone carvings of women displaying their enlarged genitals. They may well have been intended as a warning against lust, or to put people off the idea of sex and carnality. It is also likely that they served as protective 'amulets' against spells and associated evil. The figures were often built high up on a castle or mill building. There was an enduring belief right  into the middle ages that a representation of a female fertility goddess could bring good harvest and protect against the evil eye.

ROUND TOWERS

Along with illuminated manuscripts and high crosses, round towers are traditional icons of Irish identity. Since the early nineteenth century, these remarkable and finely proportioned buildings have been identified as Phoenician watch towers, phallic symbols and, more prosaically, bell-towers. Recent writings suggest that they were prestigious symbols of royal authority and the first real attempts at architecture higher than one storey.

They have a tremendous physical presence and may have been shrines in themselves, an alternative to relics of saints, but embodying elements of architecture derived from the holy city of Jerusalem. They were probably a form of sceptre, a sign of prestige for the local dynasty and were almost certainly not built exclusively as a refuge from the

Vikings. They remain powerful statements to the evolving nature of ritual and the representation of power in early Christian Ireland.

ARDMORE, CO. WATERFORD

This striking round tower was part of a monastery founded by St Declan, perhaps as early as the fifth century. The church contains two Ogham stones, one of which has the inscription 'Neta-Segamonas', which could be translated as either 'for the grandson of Segmon' or 'champion of Segomas', a Gaulish war god. Waterford and its tribal group, the Deisi, were connected to the Eoganacht of Cashel and both had long associations with Roman Britain, where Ogham writing, based on Latin, began.

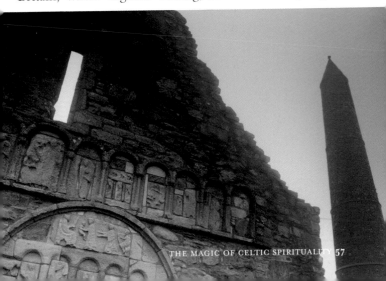

KILMACDUAGH, CO. GALWAY

The highest tower in Ireland can be seen at the monastic site of Kilmacduagh; it is more than thirty-four metres tall and dates from the late eleventh or early twelfth century. The saintly Colman, who founded this monastery, was by all accounts a 'shining' child; the story of his birth being accompanied by prophecies and attempted murder. The tale of the founding of his monastery is a bizarre tale of flying banquets, magic spells and plots being thwarted, illustrating the 'paganesque' imagination of these early writers.

EPILOGUE

The practices and beliefs of the 'new' Christian religion varied between communities, so synods were held in Arles in 314 and Rimini in 359 to formulate a universal set of beliefs acceptable to all. One popular system of belief, Pelagianism, which denied original sin, granted unbaptised dead infants access to paradise and claimed primacy for free will, was particularly detested by Rome. Pelagius was either an Irish or Welsh Celt and his teachings were especially popular in these islands and it was to refute his apparently humane teachings that Pope Celestine authorised a bishop named Palladius to come to Ireland around 430 AD and drive out the so-called heresy, thereby bringing the Irish Church back under centralised control. Ultimately, Roman Catholicism replaced all the varieties of paganism and early Christianity and as the religion of the Roman Empire, it absorbed the other attributes of Rome and became part of a network of culture, power and wealth incorporating a doctrine of centralised authority.

But how is one to tap into a sense of Celtic Spirituality today outside of organised 'groups' or activities?

It can be accessed just by choosing one of the sites from this book, somewhere you can listen to that inner voice.

It's preferable to prepare before you go, perhaps by having a light breakfast and leaving the music, phone and radio off when driving.

Always explore the site, finding the spot where you feel 'right' and as you listen to the ambient buzz of insects, birdsong, or silence, become aware of your own internal soundtrack, the throb of your heart, your breathing. Gently fade out thoughts and conversation that flit and buzz across your consciousness.

Re-tune yourself to being just where you are and nowhere else, and just take it in.